TAPPING EARTH'S HEAT

The earth's crust has pockets of very hot rock, called magma. The heat in that rock is energy. How can we tap this energy and put it to work? The answer to that question forms the basis of this fascinating book. The author starts by explaining the natural manifestations of the earth's great heat energy—volcanoes, hot springs, fumaroles, geysers—then goes on to show how the earth's hot water, steam, and hot rock are being used to heat buildings and make electricity. Simple experiments are used to underline the scientific principles.

A fountain of lava

TAPPING EARTH'S HEAT

By Patricia Lauber

Pictures by Edward Malsberg

GARRARD PUBLISHING COMPANY
CHAMPAIGN, ILLINOIS

Photo Credits

Freelance Photographers Guild: cover, pp. 6, 30
Icelandic National Tourist Office: p. 37 (top and bottom right)
Pacific Gas and Electric Company, San Francisco, California:
   pp. 44 (both), 45
Stella Snead from Bruce Coleman, Inc.: p. 16
Ted Spiegel from Black Star: p. 37 (bottom left)
Tom Tracy from Black Star: p. 24
United States Department of Energy: pp. 2, 55
Robert A. Walsh: p. 50

Cover Photograph

The Hawaiian Islands were built by undersea volcanoes. Some of these volcanoes are still active. Here Kilauea erupts, pouring out red-hot lava, one sign of the great heat inside the earth.

Library of Congress Cataloging in Publication Data

Lauber, Patricia.
   Tapping Earth's heat.

   Includes index.
   SUMMARY: Discusses the uses of heat and energy
from volcanoes, geysers, fumaroles, and hot springs.
      1. Geothermal engineering—Juvenile literature.
2. Geothermal resources—Juvenile literature.
[1. Geothermal engineering. 2. Geothermal resources]
I. Malsberg, Edward. II. Title.
TJ280.7.L38   621.4   78-6283
ISBN 0-8116-6110-5

Contents

A new eruption takes place on the island of Surtsey, then eighteen months old.

1. Inside the Earth

The date was November 1963.

The place was the North Atlantic Ocean, near Iceland.

And something strange was happening. For three days there had been a bad smell in the air. Everywhere on the Vestmann Islands the air smelled like rotten eggs. People had searched and searched, but they could not find where the smell was coming from.

Early on the morning of November 14, a fishing boat was nearing the Vestmann Islands. Its crew noticed a strange smell. They wondered if something was wrong with the boat. The engineer checked carefully. Everything was fine.

A little later the cook saw something in the distance. Smoke was rising from the ocean. Thinking a ship must be on fire, he woke the captain.

The captain studied the smoke through his glasses. Almost at once he guessed the truth. This was not a burning ship. This was a new volcano breaking through the surface of the sea.

Days earlier a volcano had started to erupt beneath the sea. It poured out gases. They bubbled to the surface and gave the air its bad smell.

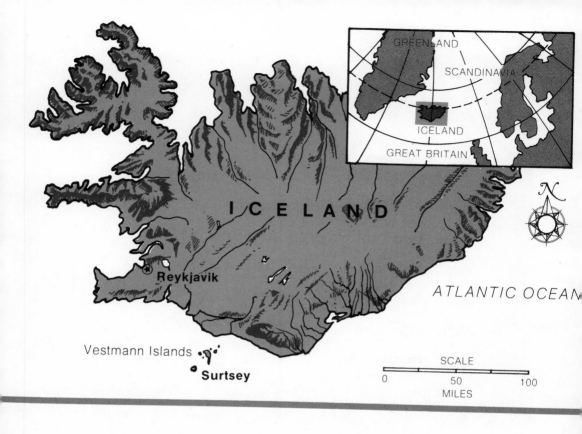

The new volcano hurled out cinder, which is bubbly rock. It hurled out the small pieces of rock called ash.

The ash and cinder piled up. They began to build a mountain. By November 15 the top of the mountain was 33 feet above the sea. Six weeks later it was 500 feet above the water. The volcano was building an island, which was named Surtsey.

The volcano went on erupting all winter. Clouds of smoke and gases rose two miles into the air. Material exploded inside the volcano. It flew into the air, then rained down on the sides of the mountain. The volcano's heat made the sea steam.

Winter storms attacked the new island. They washed away parts of it, but still the island grew.

In spring, red-hot lava began to flow. The lava covered the ash and cinder. It cooled and hardened, making a tough, thick surface. Where lava reached the sea, it formed a collar of rock. The collar kept the sea out.

The sea could not wash the island away. Surtsey had come to stay. The earth had a new volcanic island.

Where did Surtsey come from? Why did it erupt? The answers have to do with what's inside the earth.

Suppose you could take an X-ray picture of the earth. You would see that it has three main regions. They are the core, the mantle, and the crust. They are arranged like the parts of a hardboiled egg. The core is the yolk. The mantle is the white. The crust is the shell.

Earth scientists think that the core is made of iron, with a little nickel. They think that the mantle is made of dark, heavy rock. Both the core and the mantle are hotter than you can imagine. They have temperatures of thousands of degrees.

Like the eggshell, the crust is thin

and hard. It, too, is made of rock. Under the continents the crust is 20 to 30 miles thick. The crust under the oceans is only 3 to 5 miles thick.

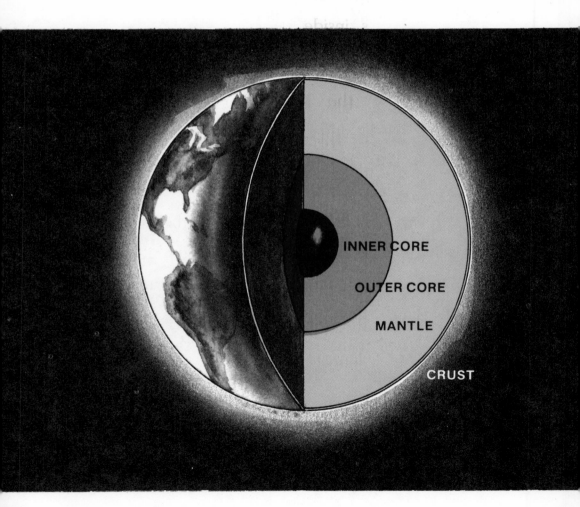

But it is made of much heavier rock.

You live on the crust, but you don't see much of it. Most of the crust is covered over with soil and sand and oceans. In a few places, though, the crust is bare. If you touched the crust, you would find it cool. But suppose you went down into the crust, into a deep mine. You would find that there is heat in the crust too. As a mine goes deeper, the temperature climbs. Some deep mines are so hot they have to be air-conditioned.

Here and there, the crust has hot spots. These are pockets of red-hot rock. This rock is so hot that it is melted, or molten. The name for this molten rock is magma. Magma is rock from the mantle that has forced its way into the crust.

The magma presses against the solid rock of the crust. Sometimes it presses against a weak spot or a crack. Then magma forces its way to the surface. A volcano erupts. The volcano may be an old one that is erupting again. Or it may be a new one, like Surtsey. Surtsey was born when magma broke through the crust under the ocean.

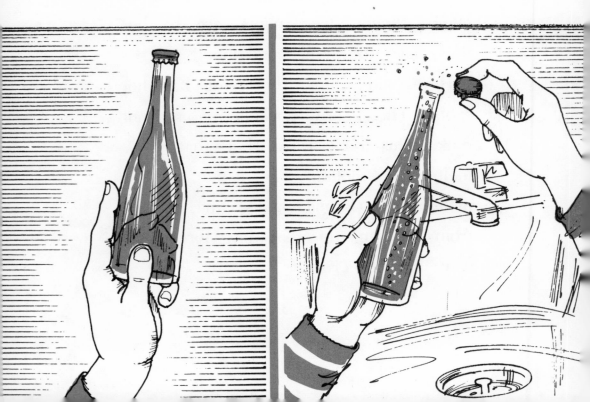

How Magma Is Like Soda Pop

Take an unopened bottle of soda pop. Hold it up to the light. Do you see bubbles?

Open the bottle and look again. Now you see bubbles. Put the cap back on the bottle. Hold the bottle over the sink and shake it gently. Remove the cap. Now look at the bubbles.

Pour a small amount of soda pop into a glass and leave it for an hour or two. (Meanwhile, drink the rest of the experiment or share it with a friend.) Come back and taste what you left in the glass. Is it flat?

What happened: Soda pop has a gas dissolved in it. The gas makes the bubbles.

You do not see bubbles in an unopened bottle. The reason is that the gas is under pressure. When you open the bottle, you release the pressure. The gas expands, taking up more space. It starts to bubble out.

Magma is something like soda pop. It has gases dissolved in it. Pressure keeps those gases dissolved. But suppose magma breaks through the crust. Then the pressure is released. The gases start to bubble out. If they bubble gently, a volcano erupts quietly. If the gases rush out, the volcano erupts violently.

By the time magma reaches the earth's surface, it has changed. It has lost its gases. And so its name also changes. It is called lava.

A volcano is a sign that the inner earth is very hot. It is a sign that huge amounts of energy are locked inside the earth, for heat is a form of energy. It has the ability to do work. The earth's great heat energy can, for

Surtsey was built by the earth's great heat energy.

example, build mountains and make volcanic islands.

There is a name for this energy. It is called geothermal energy. The word "geothermal" comes from two Greek words. One of these is *geo*, meaning "earth." You use this word every time you speak of geography. The other is *therme*, which means "heat." You use it when you speak of a thermometer.

Geothermal energy is the energy of the earth's heat.

Perhaps you have seen geothermal energy at work. You have if you've ever seen a hot spring. You have if you've ever been to see Yellowstone National Park—or even seen pictures of it. Geothermal energy heats the earth's hot springs and makes geysers erupt. Let's see how it works.

2. Earth's Teakettles

Suppose you fill a teakettle with cold water. You put it on the stove and turn on the burner. Heat from the burner spreads to the kettle to the water. With a little heat, the water warms up. With a lot of heat, it starts to boil.

That's what happens in the kitchen. It also happens in the earth. Earth, too, has teakettles—or something very much like them. Earth's teakettles are underground. They are filled with under-ground water, and they are heated by geothermal energy.

There's a lot of water underground. It is water that keeps coming from the surface. When rain falls or snow melts, some water runs off. Some sinks into the ground. It is added to water that is already underground.

Water can pass through soil. It can pass through gravel and cracks in rock. It can even pass through certain kinds of rock. But in time water reaches a bottom—material that it cannot pass through. That is why under-ground water does not just disappear into the earth. It is trapped and stored in rock, like water in a sponge.

Water near the bottom has pressure. And so it tends to spread out.

Water Has Pressure

Get an empty half-gallon milk carton and cut the top off. Punch three holes in one side. The holes should be one above the other. Try to make them the same size. You can use a nail to make the holes.

Put the carton under the faucet. Turn on the water.

When the carton is full, streams of water will shoot out all three holes. The lowest stream will shoot out farther than the middle one. And the middle one will shoot out farther than the highest one.

What happened: Water pressure increases with depth. Water near the bottom of the carton has greater pressure than water near the top, and so it shoots out farther.

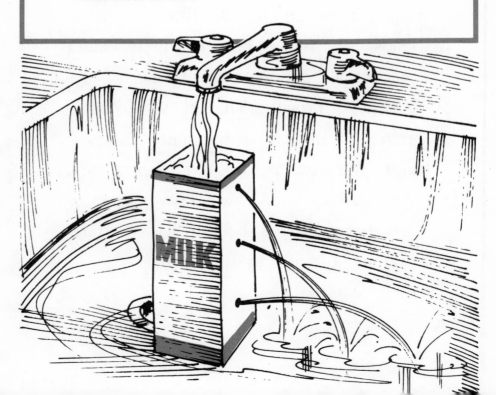

Suppose there is a place with lots of underground water. This place also has a crack or hole that leads to the surface. If there is enough pressure, water will escape through the hole. It will bubble up as a spring.

Suppose there is a lot of water, a hole, and also a pocket of magma. Then you have one of earth's teakettles. The magma heats the rock of the crust, which heats the water. The water bubbles up as a hot spring.

In a place with very little water, something else happens.

How do you test a pan to see if it is hot enough for pancakes? You don't touch it. You let a few drops of water fall on it. Remember what happens? If the pan is hot, the drops of water dance. Then in a flash they turn into steam. That is, they flash into steam. The same thing happens underground.

A place may have very hot rock and a hole that leads to the surface. But only a little water reaches the hot rock. This water will flash into steam.

When water changes to steam, it takes up more space—it expands. That is why steam rushes out the spout of a teakettle. There is not room for it inside the kettle. Pressure forces it out the spout.

The same thing happens when underground water flashes into steam. It suddenly expands. Pressure drives the steam up the opening. A hole through which steam rises is called a fumarole.

Yellowstone has many hot springs and fumaroles. But it is most famous for

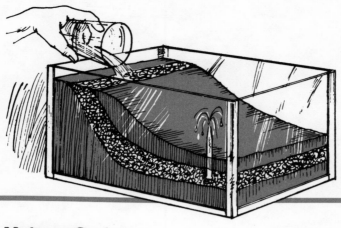

Make a Spring

This might be a good project to do at school. For it, you will need: a small aquarium tank, lots of modeling clay, pebbles (or gravel), a pencil, a medicine dropper with the top removed, a pitcher, water.

1. Make a hill in the tank, as shown in the drawing. The bottom layer of the hill is clay. The middle layer is pebbles. The top layer is clay. Be sure the top layer makes a tight seal with the glass walls of the tank. But leave the top of the hill open so that you can pour water in.

2. Test the seal by pouring water onto the top layer of clay. No water should leak into the hill. If it does, fix the leak. Pour the water out into a sink.

3. Near the bottom of the hill, make a hole with a pencil. The hole should go all the way through the clay to the pebbles. Set the dropper in the hole, wide end down. Seal the clay around the dropper.

4. Start pouring water into the pebble layer at the top of the hill. When this layer fills with water, the water will have pressure. It will escape up the dropper as a spring.

A geyser erupts at Yellowstone National Park.

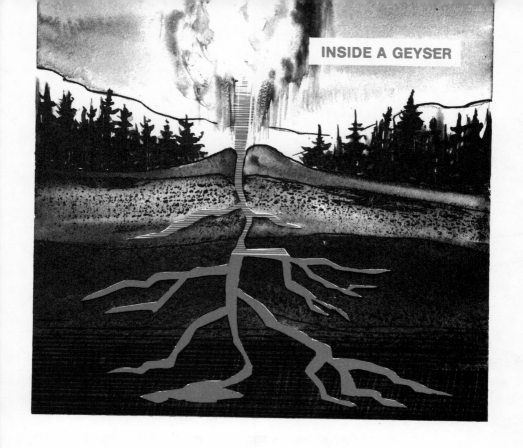

its geysers, for its fountains of hot water and steam.

A geyser is a kind of hot spring. It has a lot of underground hot water. It has an opening that leads to the surface. But a geyser's water does not bubble up steadily and gently. It erupts, dies back, and erupts again.

Hot Water Rises

You will need: a glass, a small pill bottle, water, a fountain pen with ink in it. If you don't have a fountain pen, use a dropper and any colored liquid.

Fill the glass nearly full with cold water. Fill the pill bottle about two thirds full of cold water and squirt a little ink into it. Gently lower the pill bottle into the glass. If the bottle will not stand alone, hold it.

What is happening? Nothing.

Remove the bottle and empty it. Fill it two thirds full again, but this time use hot water. Squirt in the ink and gently lower the bottle into the glass. This time an inky stream will rise out of the bottle.

What happened: Like every kind of matter, water is made of tiny particles called molecules. The molecules are constantly moving about. When water is cold, its molecules are moving fairly slowly. When water is heated, they move much faster. They jump about and spread out. They take up more space because they are farther apart. That is, hot water is less dense than cold water, and so it is lighter. That is why hot water rises.

When water is heated to the boiling point, its molecules are moving very, very fast. They jump about in every direction. Some jump right out of the water—and steam forms.

Can you think of something in the kitchen that works this way? That's right—a coffee percolator. A geyser works much the way a percolator does. Let's see what happens.

Suppose water is heating in a pan on the stove. As it warms, it starts to move. Warmer water keeps rising from the bottom of the pan. Cooler water keeps sinking from the top.

As the water reaches boiling point, bubbles keep forming near the bottom. They show that some of the water is changing to steam. The bubbles expand as they rise. When they reach the surface, they burst.

Inside a percolator, water heats as it does in a pan. But a percolator is different from a plain pan. It has a long, hollow stem with a cup-shaped foot. There is water under the foot and in the stem.

Bubbles form in the water under the foot. But they cannot move freely as they do in the rest of the percolator. They are trapped inside the foot and stem. Bubbles form, expand, and then rise suddenly, pushing water ahead of them. The water erupts, hits the glass top, and drains back over the coffee grounds. Meanwhile, more water is being forced up the stem. The coffee is perking.

A geyser is a kind of giant percolator. Instead of a metal stem, it has a long, narrow tube. Hot water and bubbles cannot move freely inside this tube. So they do not move steadily upward, as they do in the wider opening of a hot spring. A geyser erupts, stops, and then erupts again some time later.

Geysers are rare. They are found only at Yellowstone and in Iceland and New Zealand. But hot springs are common. They are found in more than 100 countries.

Every hot spring is a sign of underground hot water. It is a sign that geothermal energy is at work in nature, heating water.

Isn't there some way to put this energy to work for us? Aren't there ways for people to use geothermal energy? The answer is yes. There are several ways, some of them old and some new.

Greenhouses in Iceland are heated by the earth's hot water.

3. Tapping Earth's Hot Water

Imagine you are living in a cold land. Your house is simple. It has no plumbing, no furnace, and no stove. But near your house there is a hot spring. How can you make good use of that spring?

Hundreds of years ago, people in Iceland found some answers to that question.

They were living in a bare, northern land. Iceland was built long ago by huge floods of lava. The lava poured out of mountains beneath the sea. Perhaps you have heard of these mountains. They are part of the Mid-Atlantic Ridge, a range of mountains that runs down the middle of the Atlantic Ocean.

The ridge is a place where hot rock moves up from inside the earth. Many volcanoes erupt along the ridge. Surtsey was one of them. Lava from the ridge built the big island of Iceland.

Iceland is cold. Large parts of it are bare rock, or rock with a thin covering of soil. It has almost no trees. It has no coal, oil, or natural gas. But one of the things it does have is lots of underground hot water. You see the signs everywhere—geysers, fumaroles, and hot springs. In fact, steam accounts for the name of Iceland's capital. More than a thousand years ago, Viking ships sailed into a big bay on Iceland's coast. The Vikings saw steam rising from the land. They thought this was smoke, and so they named the place Reykjavik, which means "smoking bay."

Early Icelanders made good use of their natural hot water. They washed their clothes in hot springs. Some baked bread by burying a small oven in hot ground. A man named Snorri Sturluson went still further.

Snorri had a hot spring beside his house. The first thing he did was to make himself an outdoor bathtub near the spring. Later he piped hot water through the house to heat it. As far as anyone knows, Snorri's was the first house ever to be heated by geothermal energy. But for some reason the idea did not catch on in Iceland for another 700 years.

By the 1930s, Iceland had two big problems. It had to buy all its fuel abroad. This was expensive. In winter, thick black smoke filled the air and blanketed the city of Reykjavik. This was bad for people's health.

What could be done? Perhaps Snorri's idea would work. Iceland decided to try heating buildings with the earth's hot water. The first tests

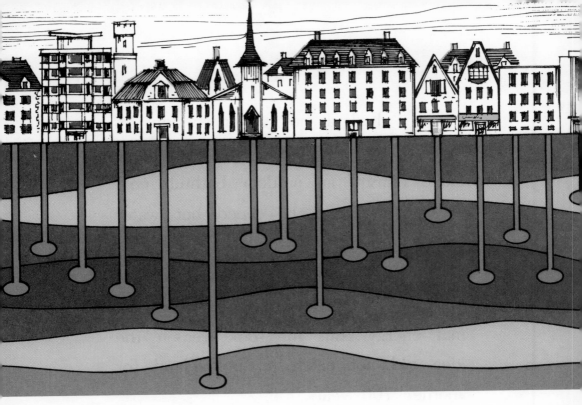

Wells under Reykjavik: The boiling point of water changes with pressure. If underground hot water is under pressure, it may be much hotter than its normal boiling point.

When a well is drilled, an opening is made. Pressure is released. Now the boiling point drops. Some hot water changes to steam. Steam and hot water erupt out of the ground as a geyser.

worked out well. Today almost every building in Reykjavik is heated with natural hot water. Iceland buys only a little fuel abroad, and its air is clean.

There are huge amounts of water under the capital. The water is very hot, and it is under pressure. To tap it, engineers drill wells through thousands of feet of lava. If they hit hot water, the pressure is released. An ear-splitting roar rattles nearby windows. A man-made geyser shoots up.

The fire department is sent for. It pumps water into the well. This water puts pressure on the hot water below. The geyser dies down. Then pumps and pipes can be put in place, and the water is stored in tanks.

Pipelines carry hot water to offices, stores, schools, churches, houses. Meters measure the amounts used. The users pay the city.

Is a room chilly? An Icelander turns the knob on a radiator. Hot water flows into the radiator and warms the room. The earth's hot water is also used in showers and baths, in dish-washers and washing machines.

The hot water warms a room by giving off some of its heat. When the water has cooled, it may be piped away and used in swimming pools. Or it may be used to cool newly tapped water that is too hot.

The earth's hot water helps feed Iceland's people. Iceland may be bare and cold, but it has big crops of cucumbers, tomatoes, and grapes. It grows flowers and even bananas. The flowers and fresh foods come from big greenhouses. And the greenhouses are heated by natural hot water.

Several other countries are also using geothermal water for heating. Among them are the Soviet Union, Hungary, France, Japan, and New Zealand. All

Iceland is a cold, northern country. But it has natural hot water swimming pools (below), and its greenhouses, heated by the earth's hot water, grow fruits, vegetables, flowers (right).

have towns where earth's hot water heats buildings, dries crops, and does other work.

A few towns in the western United States have tapped the earth's underground hot water. One is Boise, Idaho. Another is Klamath Falls, Oregon.

Geothermal water offers a fine way to heat a home. It's clean and cheap. There's just one problem. You can't use it unless you have a supply nearby. The water loses its heat when piped any distance.

But there's another way to use the earth's hot water and steam. The heat in them is energy, and one kind of energy can be changed into another kind. For example, heat energy can be changed into electrical energy, and electricity can be used miles away from the place where it was made. It can be sent through power lines to users who are hundreds of miles away.

Why Electricity Is Useful

Electricity is a useful kind of energy. It is easy to change into some other kind of energy. Look around your home and you will see many examples. Here are a few in which electricity is being changed:

into the energy of motion

into light energy

into heat energy

into the energy of sound

4. Tapping Earth's Steam

One day in 1847 an explorer was hiking through the mountains north of San Francisco. Suddenly he came upon a strange and frightening place. Steam was rising from the ground. The air smelled of sulfur. Later he told friends that he thought he had come upon the gates of hell.

But he hadn't. He had discovered the area now known as The Geysers. It is called this even though it has no geysers. Its steam comes from fumaroles.

Today you can drive up to The Geysers along a twisting, turning road. Near its end you see steam, miles of pipelines, and a giant electric power plant. The plant uses geothermal steam to make electricity.

In every power plant, some kind of energy is being changed into electrical energy. You may have visited a power plant and seen this happening.

Some plants use the energy of falling water. Somewhere high above them, water has been dammed. When it is released, it rushes down. It travels through a large pipe to the powerhouse below and spurts out through a nozzle.

The water hits the blades of a water wheel, or turbine, with great force. It makes the turbine spin—it drives the turbine. The turbine, in its turn, drives the generator. And the generator makes electricity. That's how the energy of falling water is changed to electrical energy.

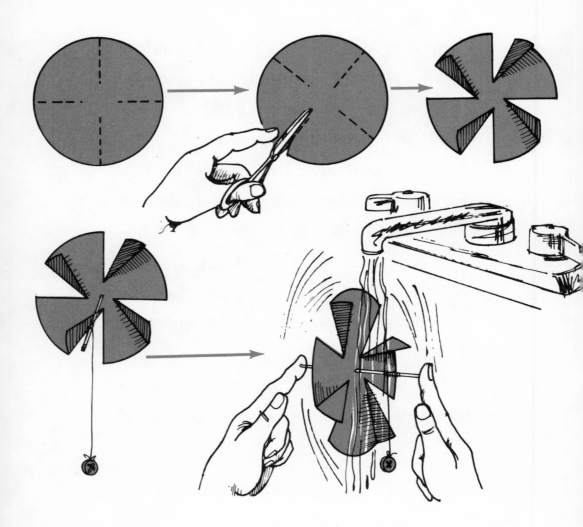

Make a Turbine

If you have ever made a pinwheel, you have made something like a turbine. When moving air catches the blades, the wheel spins.

In a real turbine, the wheel makes a shaft spin. You can make a small turbine of this kind. You will need: an empty milk carton, a compass, a ruler, a pencil, scissors, and a long, thin nail.

Cut the carton open. Using the compass, draw a circle on one of the sides. Cut out the circle.

Using your ruler, draw dotted lines as shown. Make sure the ruler touches the center of the circle.

Cut along the dotted lines. Then fold one corner of each flap as shown, to make the wheel.

Push the nail halfway through the center.

Hold the nail lightly between two fingers. Blow on the wheel. The wheel will turn and so will the shaft. Run cold water into the sink. Use it to make the wheel and shaft turn.

You can put the turbine to work. Take a short piece of string. Tie a button to one end. Tie the other end around the nail. Tie it tight. Now hold the wheel under running water. The wheel will turn and the nail will turn. The string will be wound around the nail and the button lifted. Work is being done. The energy of falling water is being used to lift a button.

Most power plants use man-made steam to drive their turbines. Water is heated in a large boiler. It is piped under great pressure to the turbine. It shoots out of the pipe as steam and drives the turbine.

To heat the water, power plants must

When a valve is turned on a wellhead at The Geysers (left), geothermal steam rushes into insulated pipelines (right)

use some kind of fuel. Most burn oil or coal or natural gas to get heat energy. Some use atomic fuel.

But a few power plants do something else. They use the earth's heat energy. They get this energy by tapping geothermal steam and hot water.

. . . and starts on its way to one of the generating plants, where the earth's heat energy is changed into electrical energy.

At The Geysers, many wells have been drilled. Some go down more than a mile. Steam rushes up the wells. It is whirled about to remove small pieces of rock. Then it is piped to the turbines. There the earth's heat energy is changed into electricity.

The world's first geothermal power plant was built at Larderello, Italy. Steam had been rising from the ground there for thousands of years. In 1904 engineers decided to try an experiment. They tapped a fumarole and used its steam to run a small generator. The generator made enough electricity to keep five light bulbs burning. The following year a geothermal power plant was built at Larderello. Today the plant is much bigger. Its electricity runs the trains in Italy.

What Spinning Does

You will need: a toy top, a shallow bowl.

Fill the bowl with just enough water to cover the top. Place the bowl in the sink. Put the top in the bowl and start it spinning. Water will fly off in all directions.

What happened: The spinning top is moving in a circle, which is a curve. Everything that moves on a curve develops a force that tends to make the thing fly away from the center. This force is called centrifugal force. When the top makes water move in a circle, drops of water fly away.

If you don't have a top, you can make the same thing happen with an eggbeater. The blades of the beater move in circles. Centrifugal force works on them, but nothing much happens. The beater is a solid, and you are holding it in place. But if you beat a bowl of water and make the water move in circles, drops of it will fly away.

If you have a clothes washer with a window, you can watch centrifugal force drying the wash. On spin-dry, the drum inside the washer spins. Everything flies away from the center. The wash is caught on the sides of the drum. But the water in the wash flies through the small holes and drains away.

Now you understand what happens when steam is whirled around at The Geysers and the little bits of rock fly away.

The wells at Larderello and at The Geysers bring up only steam. There is never any hot water mixed in with it. Steam without hot water is called dry steam. It can be piped straight to a powerhouse.

But dry steam is rare. The wells at most geothermal power plants bring up a mixture of steam and hot water. The mixture is called wet steam.

For example, there is a geothermal plant in northern Mexico which has wells that tap a supply of very hot water. As the water rises in the wells, the pressure drops. The water boils. About 20 per cent of it changes to steam. The steam is separated out and piped to the powerhouse.

Some other countries also have power plants that use wet steam. Among them are New Zealand, Japan, the Soviet Union, and the Philippines.

For years Iceland has used the energy of falling water to produce electricity. It would also like to use geothermal energy. But there is a problem. Its underground water is not hot enough to make much steam.

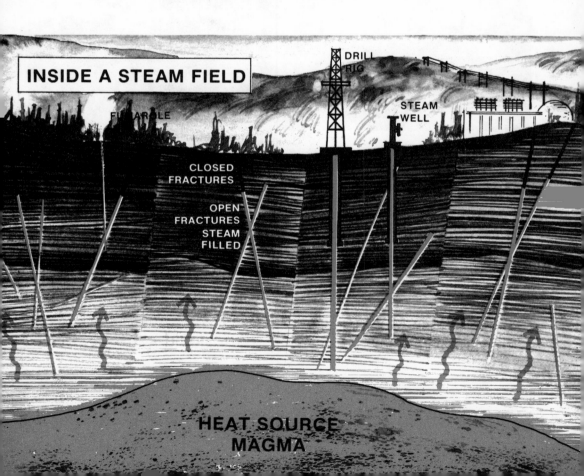

INSIDE A STEAM FIELD

DRILL RIG

STEAM WELL

FUMAROLE

CLOSED FRACTURES

OPEN FRACTURES STEAM FILLED

HEAT SOURCE MAGMA

Japanese woman uses pool of natural hot water to boil eggs.

How can this problem be solved? Here is a hint. Different liquids have different boiling points. Many boil at higher temperatures than water does. But a few boil at lower temperatures.

Do you see how to solve Iceland's problem? You can do something with water that is very hot but not making much steam. You can use its heat to make some other liquid boil—one with a lower boiling point. Then the steam of this liquid can be used to drive a turbine. And that is what Iceland is thinking of doing.

Today the earth's heat supplies only a tiny part of the world's energy needs. Some day it may supply much more. But there are many things to learn about where and how to harness the earth's heat.

5. A Look Ahead

Where can earth's heat be tapped? So far, it has been tapped mostly in places with hot springs or fumaroles. They are signs of underground energy.

These places are usually linked with volcanoes. They may have active volcanoes or dead volcanoes. Or they may have had volcanoes long, long ago. Yellowstone, for example, has no volcanoes today. But much of that high land was built by ancient out-pourings of lava. A big pocket of magma still lies under the park today.

The same places are usually linked with earthquakes. At some time, rock in the crust cracked. Surface water seeps down through the cracks. Hot water or steam may rise.

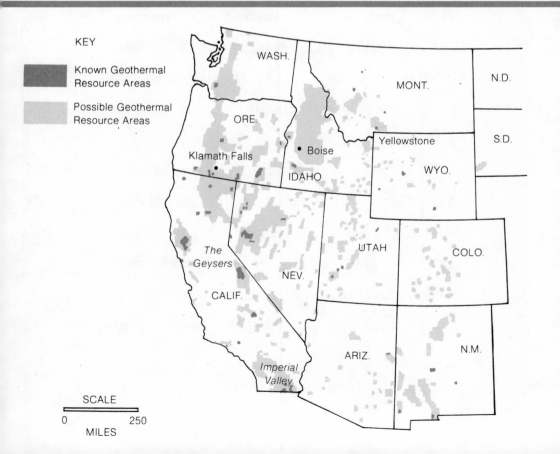

KEY

Known Geothermal Resource Areas

Possible Geothermal Resource Areas

WASH.

N.D.

MONT.

ORE

S.D.

Yellowstone

Boise

Klamath Falls

IDAHO

WYO.

UTAH

COLO.

The Geysers

NEV.

CALIF.

ARIZ.

N.M.

Imperial Valley

SCALE

0   250

MILES

Following surface clues, earth scientists have found a number of promising places to drill. There are several in California. There are many in a broad belt of land that runs from Idaho through Utah into New Mexico. Very hot water lies under Hawaii.

There is still another kind of place where earth's heat might be tapped. This kind has a pocket of magma, but it has no underground water. It has dry hot rock. Earth scientists think there are many, many places with dry hot rock.

How can anyone find these places? Are there clues that point to them? So far, earth scientists have found only a few clues. Some good ones have come from photos.

One clue is a picture taken from

space of the western states. Most of the ground was covered with snow. But there was one long bare patch. It followed a big crack in the earth. Why was this strip of land bare of snow? Scientists think heat from inside the earth melted the snow. They think this is an area of high heat flow.

Geothermal energy has melted snow in this region of California.

They think the heat comes from dry hot rock.

Some space photos have been taken with a special type of film. It picks up a kind of light that we cannot see. This is infra-red light. It is given off by anything hot. A hot iron gives off infra-red light. So does a warm engine. So does a dog. And so do some parts of the earth. These are areas with high heat flow. Infra-red photos may hold clues to dry hot rock.

Suppose you are an earth scientist. You have found a place that seems to have a lot of dry hot rock. How could you get the heat out?

There's only one way to get the heat out. You have to move it out of the rock into something else. How about moving it into water? There's no water in the ground, but you could pump some in.

You could drill a well two or more miles deep, into the dry hot rock. Next you could pump water into the well. If the water is put under great pressure, it will crack the hot rock, spread out, and be heated.

There are ways of tracking the direction of the cracks. So you could then drill a second well near their end. With luck, it will hit hot water. If not, you'll have to drill more wells to find the right place.

When you've found it, you pump cold water down the first well. The water is heated by the hot rock. Then you draw hot water up the second well and let it flash into steam.

The steam can run a turbine.

Earth scientists are testing this way of getting heat from dry hot rock. They think it's a good idea. But there is much to be learned about deep drilling. So far no one has ever drilled a hole more than five miles deep. There is much to be learned about drilling into very hot rock. It may be hot enough to melt metal.

Drilling isn't the only problem. It costs a lot of money to drill deep holes and build power plants. How long will the heat or hot water last? Will it last long enough to pay off the costs? That is hard to judge.

There are many other problems. For example, there is a huge amount of very hot water under the Imperial Valley in southern California. But the

What Happens to Metal in Salty Water

You will need: a glass, water, salt, a nail, string, a pencil.

Fill the glass about two thirds of the way up with hot water. Keep stirring in salt till no more will dissolve. Arrange the pencil, string, and nail as shown.

Put the glass in a warm, dry place out of everyone's way. Check it every day and see what happens. At the end, examine the string and nail with a magnifying glass.

What happens: As the water evaporates, the salt is left behind. It forms crystals that look like tiny ice cubes.

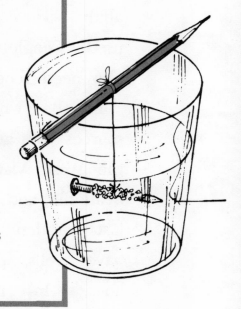

water is full of salt. In places it is ten times as salty as seawater. The salt can eat through pipes and clog machines. You can't use this water unless you can deal with the salt.

Also, the Imperial Valley is a big

farming area. Fly over it in a plane and you will see a huge checkerboard of fields of lettuce, melons, cotton, alfalfa. How can this land best be used? People need electricity. But they also need food and other crops.

In the United States most known sources of geothermal energy are in the West. Many are in places that are beautiful and wild. People love them just as they are. Should such places have wells, power plants, and power lines? In many ways, geothermal power plants are cleaner and quieter than other kinds. Even so, they can be seen, heard, and perhaps smelled. People need electricity. But they also need to get back to nature.

Still, the earth's heat energy is certain to play a part in our future. It may never meet all our energy needs. But it can be important.

Think about where most of our heat energy comes from today. It comes from burning fuels such as oil, gas, and coal. These fuels can be used up. That is why scientists are studying sources of energy we can't use up— energy from the sun, from the winds, from the waves.

One important source is the earth's heat. There is a huge amount of it beneath our feet. And the earth keeps making more.

The earth's heat comes from certain atoms, such as those in uranium. These are atoms that keep breaking down. When they do, they give off heat.

In an atomic power plant, large numbers of atoms are made to break down. They give off great heat.

Inside the earth, atoms break down naturally. For example, in a piece of uranium, some atoms are always breaking down. Nothing starts the breaking down. Nothing can stop it. It just happens.

HOW A URANIUM ATOM IS MADE TO SPLIT

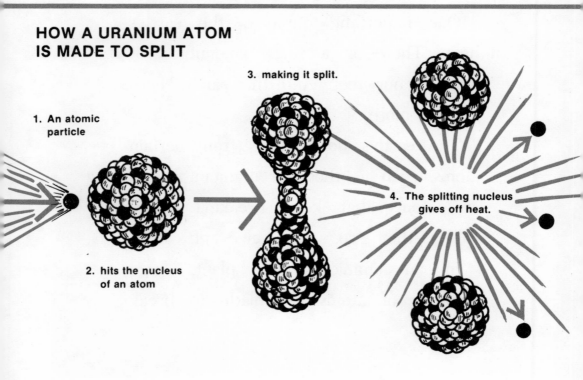

1. An atomic particle

2. hits the nucleus of an atom

3. making it split.

4. The splitting nucleus gives off heat.

When an atom breaks down, it gives off only a tiny bit of heat. But inside the earth, many, many atoms are breaking down all the time. And this has been going on for hundreds of millions of years. Little of the heat escapes. And so great heat has built up inside the earth.

In time, all the atoms that can break down will have broken down. But that day won't come for at least two billion years.

Meanwhile, the earth will stay very hot inside. Its heat is energy. Its heat is great energy, as Surtsey and other volcanoes remind us. We can learn to tap and use this energy—and that's a good thing for this energy-hungry world.

Index